Earth's Endangered Creatures

MISSION RHINO

Earth's Endangered Creatures

MISSION RHINO

Written by
Jill Bailey

Illustrated by
Alan Baker

STECK-VAUGHN
LIBRARY
A Division of Steck-Vaughn Company
Austin, Texas

*This series is concerned with the world's
endangered animals, the reasons why their numbers are
diminishing, and the efforts being made to save them
from extinction. The author has described these events
through the eyes of fictional characters. Although the
situations described are based on fact, the people and the
events described are fictitious.*

Editor: Andy Charman
Designer: Mike Jolley
Consultant: Ian Redmond

Library of Congress Cataloging-in-Publication Data

Bailey, Jill
Mission Rhino / written by Jill Bailey: illustrated by Alan Baker.
p. cm.– (Save our species)
At head of title: Earth's endangered creatures.
"A Templar book" – T.p. verso
Summary: A young African boy learns why rhinoceros are hunted
and why it is important to protect them from poachers.

ISBN 0-8114-6550-0   Softcover Binding
ISBN 0-8114-2702-1   Hardcover Library Binding
[1. Rhinoceros—Fiction. 2. Rare animals—Fiction.
3. Wildlife conservation—Fiction.]
I. Baker, Alan. ill. II. Title. III. Title: Earth's endangered
creatures. IV. Series.
PZ7.B1525M1   1990   90-32529
[Fic]—dc20   CIP AC

Color separations by Positive Colour Ltd,
Maldon, Essex, Great Britain

2 3 4 5 6 7 8 9 0 LB 96 95 94 93 92

CONTENTS

THE POACHERS' TRAIL.

In the shimmering heat of the African dry season, a 12-year-old boy and a 78-year-old man sat at the foot of an old tree. The older man, Walter, had once taken his good friend **Joshua Msumo** into the bush to show him the animal tracks and signs. Together they had watched the impalas feeding and the weaver birds building nests. Walter was now too old to go into the bush, but Joshua was eager to learn more.

"Tell me about the black rhinos," he pleaded. "Do they really wear armor?"

Old Walter laughed.

"No," he replied, "but they do have very tough hides. They need good protection as they push their way through the thornbush. They also fight each other, and those horns can give even a rhino hide quite a nasty scrape. Old rhinos are covered in scars."

"How big do their horns grow?" asked Joshua.

"The front one is the larger of the two," said Walter. "It may be up to 19½ inches long. The longest one I've heard of was over 53 inches long. "

"Why are the horns so valuable?" asked Joshua.

"The Yemenis make dagger handles out of them," Walter explained, "and in Asia, rhino horn is believed to be a cure for fevers and all sorts of other illnesses. Now there are very few rhinos and the price has gone higher and higher. African rhino horn can be worth over $11,000 a pound. That is three times more than the same weight of gold."

Joshua suddenly realized that he wanted to see a rhinoceros up close for himself.

The population of black rhinos has fallen from 15,000 in 1980 to fewer than 4,000 today. This is almost entirely due to hunting by poachers.

A food store in a village in the Luangwa valley, Zambia. In this village, as in Joshua's, the main crop is corn.

Walter and Joshua sat at the foot of the old tree and talked. Walter could remember a time when there were many more rhinos.

"What do rhino tracks look like?" asked Joshua. He wanted to know more about the rhinos.

Walter took his walking stick and drew a large footprint on the ground.

"Rhinos have only three toes," he explained, "but each is very big, so the rhino's weight is evenly spread out. Rhinos usually use the same paths, which they make themselves. Once you have found the tracks, they are fairly easy to follow. When you are older, you can track them yourself."

Walter got slowly to his feet.

"I must go now," he said.

Joshua wandered home, still thinking about the rhinos. He was hungry, but food had been scarce recently. From time to time, Joshua's father went on a secret trip. When he came back, he had plenty of money, and the family was able to buy fresh meat in the market and sometimes school books. As he entered the thatched hut, his mother signaled to him to be quiet. He could hear deep voices behind the curtain. When she turned back to her cooking, Joshua crept up to it.

He heard voices, but only recognized his father's. The men were discussing hunting rhinos in the morning.

Rhinos usually follow the same route to and from water. Egrets often accompany them, feeding on insects disturbed by the rhinos.

The curtain moved, and Joshua leapt quickly out of the way. His father came out with two men, and they disappeared into the sunlight. Joshua decided he would get up early and follow them in the morning when they went to look for rhinos.

9

Miombo "bush" in Zambia. Black rhinos browse at the edges of such wooded areas in central Africa.

Right: *In many parts of Africa people live in large families. Land for so many is often hard to find.*

The stars were just fading from the sky as Joshua crept out of the hut to follow the hunters. It was too dark to see their footprints. He would have to stay close to them until the sun was higher.

The men passed through the fields that Joshua's family owned. His grandfather's farm had been divided among six brothers. Now none of the farms was large enough to support a family, especially one as large as Joshua's. Only these mysterious trips of his father's kept the family clothed and fed.

Joshua followed the men across the river, being careful not to splash. It was a long trek into the thornbush. Three hours later, in the blazing sun, he heard two shots in the distance.

Joshua crept forward slowly. Soon he found the rhino tracks in the sand. They became mingled with the hunters' footprints. Then he saw that the grasses and bushes all around were trampled and broken and spotted with blood. He stopped to listen. The men's voices were now fading into the distance. He followed the bloodstains, and there it was – a huge rhino, lying dead in the sun.

Joshua stared in amazement. Could this be the animal they had nicknamed "The Thunderer"? Blood was trickling from the bullet holes in its side. On the rhino's snout there was a jagged ring of skin around a sawed-off stump. This was where the magnificent horn had been. Without it, the animal seemed less like a mighty beast, and more like a huge pile of meat from a butcher.

To his surprise, Joshua felt sorry for the rhino. It didn't seem right that it should die like this, in a crater of red soil formed by its own fall, left alone to rot in the sun. Such a great animal should have a proper burial, with music, dancing, and feasting.

Joshua remembered his uncle's funeral, and the anger they had felt toward the game scouts who had shot him. Joseph Msumo had died because he had broken the law by killing a rhino. The game scouts found him with his kill. As they approached, he shot at them. The scouts fired back and Joseph fell dead beside the rhino. Joshua frowned. Wasn't a man's life worth more than a rhino's life? After all, his tribe had hunted wild animals on this land for as long as anyone – even 78-year-old Walter – could remember.

The rhino lay dead in a crater of red soil. The horn had been cut from its head, and the rest of the body left to rot.

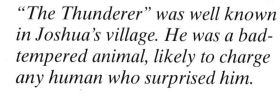

"The Thunderer" was well known in Joshua's village. He was a bad-tempered animal, likely to charge any human who surprised him.

Joshua crept forward and touched the rhino's warm skin. His father and the other men could not be far away. After a few minutes, Joshua found their tracks in the red soil. He wanted to get close enough to watch the next kill. His eye caught a red and yellow paper cylinder – an empty gun cartridge case. He slipped it into his pocket.

The ground was baked hard by the sun, and the tracks were very faint. Then Joshua found more rhino footprints leading into some bushes. They looked very fresh.

He began to follow them. Suddenly, he heard a crunching sound. He looked up and saw a rhino eating twigs very close to him. Joshua froze. Then he heard the sound of men's voices coming straight toward him. Forgetting the rhino, he turned and ran in the opposite direction as fast as he could.

Black rhinos are browsers. They feed on the thornbush, and help to prevent it from spreading across the savanna.

There was a furious snort, then a great thrashing and crashing as the rhino charged out of the undergrowth toward him. Joshua climbed up the nearest tree, grazing his hands and legs on the rough branches. He made it just in time; his heart was beating fast. The rhino was right behind him. Head down, it charged into the tree, using its horn like a battering ram. The tree shook. A shot rang out. The rhino started, bellowed, then swung around and rushed away.

Joshua clung desperately to the tree. When the rhino butted the trunk, the tree shook. It wouldn't hold him for long.

There was a crash of breaking bushes, then a thud as the wounded rhino fell to the ground. Joshua's father and his companions burst angrily into the open below the boy's tree.

"How dare you follow us?" shouted his father. "You could have been killed."

Joshua clambered down from his tree.

"I'm sorry," he said. "I wanted to see the rhino." Then he had an idea. "I found this." He fished out the gun cartridge and handed it to his father. "You should be more careful – you could be caught by the game scouts." His father calmed down.

"You'd better come with us," he said.

The men went over to the rhino and cut out the horn. Later that afternoon they made their way toward a distant village. Just outside the village they stopped under a large tree and waited. Soon, a truck drew up beside them. Two tall, dark men got out and approached them. They were horn dealers from Somalia. The horns were handed over for a lot of money. Then the men drove off.

"What will they do with the horns?" he asked.

"They will take them to a place called Mpulungu, on Lake Tanganyika," said one of the hunters. "A fishing boat takes them to Burundi, where exporting rhino horn is legal. Then they can be sent to North Yemen in Arabia, where they will be carved

In North Yemen, every Muslim man wears a dagger in his belt.

Left: *The dealers bought the horns from Joshua's father to sell for larger sums of money.*

into dagger-handles. To the Yemenis, a rhino horn dagger-handle is a sign of importance and wealth. They have been wearing daggers like this for hundreds of years."

Joshua and the hunters returned to their own village.

"We want to talk man's talk," said his father. "Go home, Joshua, and have your supper."

John, a boy of Joshua's age, was visiting for supper. He told Joshua and his mother that many of the men in his village were employed as game scouts to protect the rhinos.

Parks have been set up all over Africa, not only to protect rhinos, but other animals as well, such as these lions.

"People from all over the world pay lots of money to see rhinos and other big animals, like elephants and lions," he said.

"Don't they shoot them?" asked Joshua.

"Not any more," replied John. "They take pictures. The animals are protected in a game reserve, like they are here, but there are more scouts. They keep poachers away and take the tourists to the rhinos. The tourists' money has paid for my school. In the next village it paid for a beautiful health clinic and medicine."

"I'd like to take pictures of rhinos," said Joshua.

John laughed. "You can't afford to be a tourist," he said, "but you could work as a scout. Then you'd be out every day looking for rhinos. You would earn more than if you stayed on the farm. Scouts have smart uniforms, too."

Tourists pay a lot of money to see the rhinos. Many of the local people can share the benefits of this money.

DANGEROUS WORK

David Mapoma was a bright young man. He had done well at school, and his teachers had said he should look for work in Lusaka, Zambia's capital city. But after a few months in an office, David was homesick for the bush. He had returned to the village and gotten a job as a game scout in the local game reserve. He had just been promoted, and was now training his first anti-poaching patrol.

David looked at the eager young recruits before him.

"I hope you all know how to use a gun," he said to them. "These poachers can be dangerous."

"We have only three rounds of ammunition each," protested one of the scouts. "They will soon out-shoot us."

"We cannot afford more ammunition," said David. "That is why you must take the poachers by surprise. If they kill all of the rhinos, you will have no more work."

"Better no job than no life," muttered the nervous scout.

"The bush is your heritage," replied David sharply. "Your fathers and grandfathers and great-grandfathers hunted the game on this land. Already the poachers have killed so many animals that hunting is no longer worthwhile. The money will come from the tourists only if there are animals to see. You are defending your birthright and your children's future."

Left: *An anti-poaching patrol gets ready for action. Arresting poachers is dangerous work. Game scouts have to be good trackers and brave men.*

Black rhinos in a national park. Today, poaching and the farming of formerly wild areas are endangering the populations of most of the larger animals.

The next day, David and some of his scouts set out to visit a remote part of the Reserve to make a count of the rhinos. They took with them Kurt Wagner, a German zoologist who was studying rhinos. David needed to know how many rhinos were left in the area, and whether their numbers were increasing or decreasing. The Reserve could afford only a few full-time game scouts and David wanted to send them to the areas where the rhinos were most in danger.

It was a long, tiring journey. Finally, they set up camp near a partly dried-up riverbed. The following morning they set off at dawn. The rhinos had begun to forage at dawn, coming out of the thickets and patches of forest where they spent the night. By noon they would be resting and difficult to see. Already the elephants were on the move, padding silently toward the river in the early morning haze.

After several hours of looking, one of the scouts, Ben Mwanza, signaled that he had found some tracks. They were very faint, but beside them sat some fresh dung. The rhino had been there that morning. Soon the ground became stony, and the tracks disappeared, so they searched

David and the scouts spent many hours searching for the rhinos. They followed some tracks for a while and then one of the scouts signaled to the others to stand still. He had spotted the rhino.

for broken twigs to show where the rhino fed as it walked. Then Ben waved at them. He had spotted the gray-brown back of the rhino in the distance.

In the early morning sun the elephants made their way to the river. Since they do not sweat, both rhinos and elephants need to visit water regularly to stay cool.

David wanted to get closer to see the animal's size. He also wanted to know if it was a bull or a cow (male or female), and whether it had any features like large or curving horns to help him recognize it if he came across it in the future.

Ben was worried. The wind was blowing their scent toward the rhino. Quietly, they crept around to approach it from the other side. There they found many more tracks.

"Rhinos are creatures of habit, David whispered. "They like to have their midday rest and their evening drink at the same places, so they wear paths between them."

The track led through some dense undergrowth, forming a low tunnel, about the height and width of an adult rhino. The men had to bend down to enter it.

A large cow and her three-months-old calf stood in front of them. The calf was suckling, reaching up to his mother's teats, warm with milk. The men did not stay long to watch. Female rhinos with calves are extremely

A rhino calf can weigh up to 88 pounds at birth. It will stay with its mother for two to three years, but she will drive it away when she produces her next calf.

Rhinos visit water to drink in the early morning and in the evening. In dry areas, they travel up to nine miles to find water.

dangerous and will charge if they sense danger. At any moment the wind might change and carry their scent toward her.

It was midday and the sun was hot, so they stopped for a drink. This was the most risky time for stalking. The rhinos were resting in the long grass or in the bushes, and it was easy to come up on one unexpectedly and surprise it. A rhino whose sleep has been disturbed is likely to be very bad-tempered.

An hour later, they heard puffing and snorting, and a clash of horns in the distance. David and Kurt saw through their binoculars a bull rhino chasing a cow. The bull stopped to spray the nearby bushes with urine. Then he scraped at the ground, and bashed the bushes with his horns. He began to circle the cow, which immediately charged him. He retreated, rubbed his nose on the ground, and scraped with his feet. Then he advanced, holding his tail stiffly in the air. The two rhinos stood nose to nose, swinging their heads from side to side and scraping with their hind feet. This was repeated many times, until finally the cow stood still while the bull laid his head tenderly on her rump. Soon they would mate, and in 15 months' time there would be a new calf.

After a week, David and Kurt had found about 20 rhinos. They had also collected 13 rhino skulls, carefully marking on the map the place where each skull had been found. Only two of the skulls were undamaged. These were from old

Bull and cow rhinos often fight in the early stages of courtship. The bull snorts, twists his tail, and stamps on the ground.

animals with worn teeth. They had died naturally. The rest had knife cuts or axe marks where the poachers had cut out the horns. There were also several very young animals among them. They could not have had very large horns.

"The poachers are desperate," said David angrily. "They're shooting every animal they can."

Skulls from poached rhinos show clearly where the horns have been removed. These are from the Laikipia ranch in Kenya.

David, Kurt, and the scouts drove back to the Reserve headquarters, pleased to have found so many rhinos still surviving. As David took the skulls to the Reserve's small museum, he noticed John and Joshua looking at the rhino photographs.

"This is why the tourists come," said John. "They want to take home pictures like these for their friends to admire."

Just then, the anti-poaching patrol returned, marching seven poachers in handcuffs before them. Joshua started. He feared his father might be among them, but he tried not to look too concerned.

"Are they from your village?" Joshua asked.

"No," replied John. "We know that if we keep the animals, there will be money for schools and clinics for our children and grandchildren. If we shoot them, there will only be money for a few poachers now."

David overheard the earnest young boy. He went over to talk to John and Joshua.

"Do you like rhinos?" he asked.

"Yes," replied Joshua. "I think so."

David glanced at his watch. The sun would be setting soon.

"Come with me," he said, and he led them to his Land Rover. They rattled and bumped over the rough path until they were almost at the river. Then David stopped the Land Rover.

At the Reserve headquarters Joshua and John were looking at photographs of elephants and rhinos. They had been taken by tourists.

This rhino has died after a fight with another rhino. Rangers are removing its horn before it can be stolen and illegally sold to dealers. It is important not to encourage trade in horns.

Trade in rhino horn is illegal in most African countries. This warehouse in Nairobi contains horns that have been confiscated by the Kenyan government.

"In a few years' time, you may not be able to see rhinos any more," said David. "There will be hardly any left."

"Is that because of the poachers?" asked Joshua.

"Mainly," said David, "but it's also because a lot of the rhino's wild home has been cleared to make way for new farms."

"Can't you save the rhinos?" asked Joshua.

"We're trying to," said David. "In some reserves we have very high electric fences to keep the poachers out. We are removing some of the rhinos to these safe places. If they breed well there, maybe later we can take some of them back to the wild. That was how we saved the white rhino from extinction. There are also rhinos safe and breeding well in zoos. In many countries it is now legal to shoot poachers on sight."

Joshua shuddered.

"It would be much better," David continued, "if we could stop people who buy the horn. It won't be easy. It means changing attitudes that are centuries old."

The southern race of the white rhinoceros was once almost extinct. There is now a thriving population of over 3,000 animals.

"At this time of day, a very old rhino comes to drink here," he said. "Watch and listen."

They waited. Eventually the old rhino came plodding down the path. Joshua leaned forward and almost fell off his seat. The rhino looked toward them. Then it continued on its way.

"Do you think it saw us?" asked Joshua, feeling a bit guilty.

"No," said David. "Rhinos are very shortsighted. It may have heard us. Rhinos rely on hearing and smell to find their way around and to warn them of danger."

"His skin looks too big," giggled Joshua. "Has he shrunk with age?"

Joshua thought of old Walter's shriveled body and the folds of skin around his face.

"No, that's just how it is," said David. "He's not as big as the white rhino, but he could still weigh 2,200 to 3,300 pounds."

Joshua stared and stared at the rhino. He thought it was the most beautiful and magical animal he had ever seen.

Rhinos wallow in mud almost every day. The mud helps them to keep cool and protects their skin against insect bites.

MISSION
RHINO

Kurt Wagner leaned out of the cockpit of the helicopter and carefully aimed his binoculars. A black rhino, alarmed by the helicopter, had broken cover and was charging across the open grassland of the savanna.

Two years earlier Kurt had been awarded his doctorate in zoology from Frankfurt University in Germany. He had studied rhinos ever since. Today he was going to help the game scouts move several rhinos to another part of the Reserve. There had been a lot of poaching in this area recently and the rhinos were not safe.

Kurt looked down at the plains, a patchwork of dry grasses and dense thickets of spiny shrubs and scattered thorn trees. This was where the rhinos were sheltering.

Black rhinos are almost six and a half feet high, and can reach the lower branches of the trees to

The black rhino has a long upper lip which it uses to grasp twigs and leaves. This feature is typical of browsing animals.

Left: *The noise of the helicopter flushed the rhino out of its hiding place and onto the open grassland.*

browse. They curl their upper lip around small twigs and strip off the leaves.

Once there had been hundreds of rhinos in this part of the Reserve, but European hunters killed many of them in the early part of this century. Now the poachers were killing the few that were left. Any rhino that showed itself during the day was likely to be shot. They stay hidden in the undergrowth, making them difficult to find.

Kurt found only a few black rhinos over a large area. No wonder they were not breeding well. Black rhinos are unsociable animals. Except for young rhinos who have just left their mothers, they tend to live alone for most of the time. With so few rhinos left, it was difficult for cows to meet bulls during the few days each month when they were ready to mate.

Now that Kurt had discovered where the rhinos were, the game scouts, who were expert trackers, could set out quietly on foot to find them. But first he needed to set up camp. Eventually he spotted a partly dried up riverbed. There was still a trickle of water. This would be a good place.

The rhino rescue patrol set out in a convoy of trucks and jeeps. They were carrying enough food for a month, dart guns with tranquilizers, lamps, two-way radios, tents, campbeds, axes, and a special truck for moving the rhinos. This truck had a sleigh – a large platform of wood mounted on steel runners – that could be hauled up into the truck. This would be used for loading the rhinos onto the truck.

Three game scouts and 30 helpers recruited from the Reserve staff would assist David and Kurt.

"Why do we need so many men?" asked one of the recruits.

"Rhinos are so heavy," replied David, "we'll need all these men to haul them onto the truck."

Right: *Black rhino bulls live alone but may be part of a group that visits the same waterhole. They have their own feeding areas and rarely fight each other.*

Rhinos are very difficult to spot. Here an antenna is being used to locate rhinos that have been fitted with a radio collar.

The party reached the campsite and began to build a large stockade. They cut down trees and made thick stakes. They hammered these into the soil to form several pens, each with a heavy gate on ropes which could be lowered into place by people on top of the stockade.

On the first day they followed a large rhino's trail to the river. The rhino was feeding quietly in a clump of mopane trees. Now they

The stockade has to be strong. When cornered, a rhino will charge at the posts, the scouts, and even the rhino in the next pen, ramming the wood with its horn.

had to tranquilize the rhino so that they could move it back to the camp and the stockade.

This was a dangerous task. David and Ben crept forward, each carrying a gun armed with a dart full of tranquilizer. Another scout carried an ordinary gun in case the rhino should charge. The rest of the party climbed into some nearby trees, out of danger.

David inched forward. He had to get within about 100 feet in order to hit the rhino with a dart. He shook a little dust into the wind. It blew toward him. This meant that his smell was not being carried to the rhino. The rhino was a perfect target, standing sideways before him. David fired. The great beast started in alarm, then charged away through the bushes.

"After it," cried David.

The scouts and trackers climbed down from their trees and ran after the rhino. It charged over a steep hill, into a gully, across a dry riverbed, and up another hill. They must have chased it for about two miles before it finally began to stagger and eventually sank to the ground.

The rhino was feeding. David and Ben crept toward it, each with his tranquilizer gun loaded and ready to fire. If the rhino detected them, it would probably charge.

The rhino lay on its stomach.

"We must turn it on its side," said David. "It's not good for it to lie on its stomach like this."

They tied ropes around its snout, belly, and legs. Several men on each rope heaved and tugged until the rhino finally rolled to its side.

The rhino measured nearly 13 feet from head to tail and about $5\frac{1}{2}$ feet from foot to shoulder. Kurt checked the rhino's heartbeat with a stethoscope while David took its body temperature.

The rhino was getting hot, so David lay some cut branches over it. Then he radioed to the camp for the truck.

About 40 minutes later the truck appeared, bumping over the rocks.

"Won't the rhino wake up soon?" asked one of the recruits.

"The dart usually works for about five hours," said David, "perhaps less for such a big rhino."

They lowered the sleigh to the ground, then strained together to heave 5,300 pounds of sleeping rhino onto it. They tied the rhino down so that it wouldn't be able to hurt anyone if it woke up.

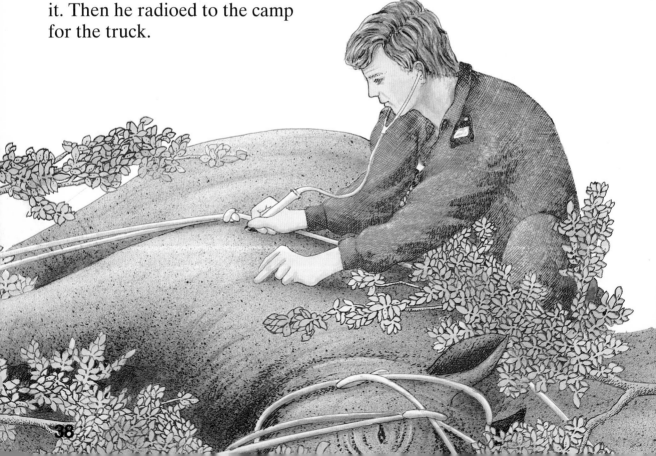

Drugged rhinos are loaded onto a special sleigh. This is then hoisted onto a truck. It takes a lot of men to lift a rhino.

Kurt checked the rhino's heartbeat with his stethoscope. David cut some branches from a nearby bush and lay them over the rhino to keep it cool.

The truck moved slowly back to camp so as not to injure the rhino. David, Kurt, and Ben sat in the back watching the rhino. Suddenly, it lifted its head.

"Look out!" cried David.

The rhino lashed out with its bound feet and hit Kurt. He toppled over the side.

"Are you all right?" shouted David.

Kurt struggled to his feet.

Rhinos reproduce very slowly. A calf will stay with its mother for about three years until she mates and produces another calf. Over-hunting endangers this slow-breeding species.

"Yes, thanks, just a few bruises." He climbed back onto the truck.

"We'd better hurry," said David. "The rhino's waking up."

When they reached the camp, they backed the truck up to the stockade, and slid the sleigh into one of the pens. Kurt and David loosened the knots tying the rhino's feet. Then they both climbed out and up the side of the stockade.

The rhino was very angry. It charged the posts, shaking David and Kurt violently. After several charges, David threw a small stone into a pan of water in one corner of the pen to distract it.

The rhino turned to charge at the noise, then noticed the water and settled down for a welcome drink.

When they had several rhinos in the pens, David radioed to headquarters for a truck to carry them one by one to their new home.

Kurt and David climbed the sides of the stockade and looked down at the rhino. It was very angry and charged at the posts. The stockade shook from top to bottom.

As they traveled to the rhinos' new home, one of the scouts asked, "Who pays for all this?"

"The government puts in some money," David replied, "but we get overseas help through the World Wide Fund for Nature, from SAFE – Save Endangered African Wildlife – in America, the Rhino Rescue Trust in London, and many others."

Turning to Kurt, David said, "Tell us about your trip to Thailand."

"As you know," began Kurt, "many people in Asia use Chinese medicines. Some of these medicines are made from rhino horn, others use its skin, and even its dung and urine. Sometimes the patient mixes powdered horn with water or milk to make a drink. Most often it is mixed with herbs. It is said

In countries such as China, Japan, and Korea, rhino horn shavings are made into medicines. This has been going on for centuries.

to cure toothache, back pain, fever, and many other illnesses. People have been taking this mixture for thousands of years, although there is no scientific proof that it can cure anything!"

"I thought it was used as an aphrodisiac – a love potion," said David.

"Only in a few parts of northern India," replied Kurt. "The medicine trade is the most important cause of the rhino's decline. That's where most of the horn goes."

"How can we stop it?" asked one of the scouts.

"In many places we are convincing people that other kinds of horn, such as saiga antelope horn, are just as good," replied Kurt. "Most Asian countries have banned imports of rhino horn, and it is becoming very expensive."

"What about the dagger-handles?" asked David

"That trade is still strong," said Kurt, "but the outlook is promising. The North Yemen government banned the import of horn in 1982 and made it illegal to carve horn. In any case, Yemeni men are adopting western habits, and fewer of them carry daggers today.

Protecting such a shy, solitary animal as the black rhino is difficult. Saving it requires the support of people the world over.

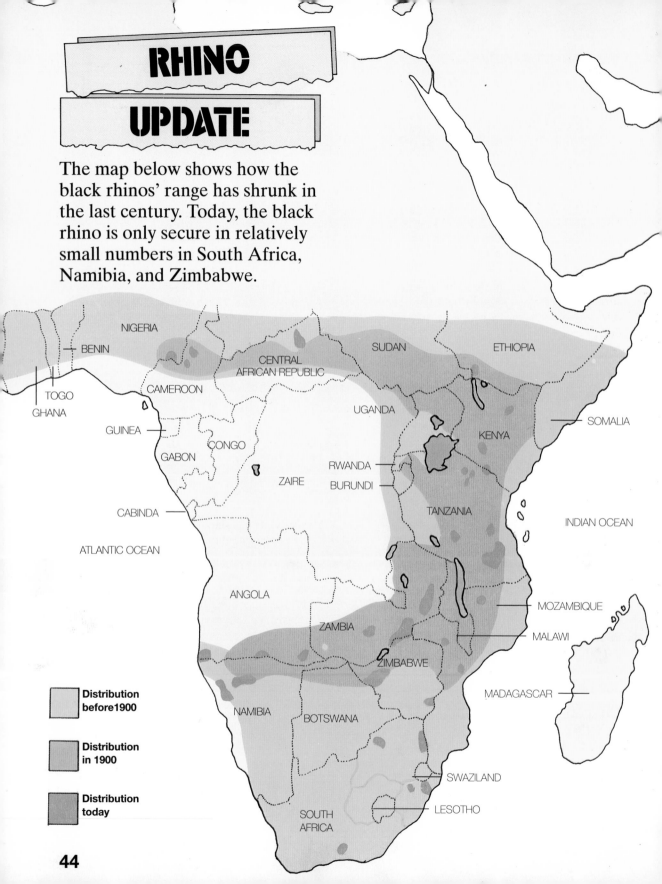

RHINO

UPDATE

The map below shows how the black rhinos' range has shrunk in the last century. Today, the black rhino is only secure in relatively small numbers in South Africa, Namibia, and Zimbabwe.

NIGERIA

BENIN

TOGO

GHANA

GUINEA

CAMEROON

CENTRAL AFRICAN REPUBLIC

SUDAN

ETHIOPIA

UGANDA

SOMALIA

KENYA

CONGO

GABON

ZAIRE

RWANDA

BURUNDI

CABINDA

TANZANIA

INDIAN OCEAN

ATLANTIC OCEAN

ANGOLA

ZAMBIA

MOZAMBIQUE

MALAWI

ZIMBABWE

MADAGASCAR

NAMIBIA

BOTSWANA

SWAZILAND

LESOTHO

SOUTH AFRICA

Distribution before 1900

Distribution in 1900

Distribution today

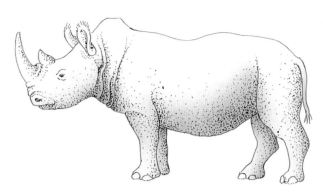

The Black Rhino • The black rhino can be 13 feet long and stand 5 feet 11 inches high at the shoulder. It has two horns and a gray or brown coat . The black rhino lives in tropical forests and scrub, browsing on twigs and leaves. It survives in scattered populations from South Africa in the south to Somalia in the north. Fewer than 4,000 black rhinos remain.

The White Rhino • This large rhino can be 13 feet 8 inches long and stand 6 feet 7 inches high It has two horns; the front one can grow 6^1/$_2$ feet or more. The white rhino is not really white – its name comes from the Afrikaans word *weit,* meaning "wide," which refers to its wide mouth. It has smooth gray skin and eats grass. About 3,000 remain.

The Javanese Rhino • The Javanese rhino grows to 11^1/$_2$ feet long and 5 feet 11 inches high. It has a scaly skin. Only bulls have a horn, which seldom grows more than 10 inches long. The Javanese rhino lives in forests, where it feeds on twigs and fruit. In the last century it was hunted almost to extinction, and today there are only about 50 animals left.

The Sumatran Rhino • This is the smallest rhino, measuring 9 feet 2 inches long and 4 feet 11 inches high. The Sumatran rhino has gray, hairy skin and ears. It is a browser, and lives in mountain rain forests in southeast Asia. It is seldom seen, coming out to feed at dawn and dusk. It is thought that between 530 and 960 Sumatran rhinos remain.

The Indian Rhino • This is the largest rhino, measuring up to 13 feet 9 inches long and 6^1/$_2$ feet high. It has one horn of up to 24 inches long, and knobby gray skin that hangs in folds. It feeds mainly on grass. The Indian rhino once roamed northern India, Pakistan, Nepal, and Bangladesh. Today it is mostly found in national parks. Fewer than 1,800 remain.

INDEX